# Tennessee

# Mountain Man

~~~~~~~~~~~~~~~~~~

# Nick Grindstaff

By

## Patti Clark

# Tennessee Mountain Man

## By

## Patti Clark

# CHARACTERS

*NICK GRINDSTAFF~The legendary hermit that lived in the East Tennessee mountains alone for over thirty years.

*MARY HEATON GRINDSTAFF~Nick Grindstaff's Mother.

*ISSAC GRINDSTAFF~ Nick Grindstaff's Father.

*BENJAMIN WILSON~A man Nick went to for help.

*BAXTER McEWEN~The man who found Nick dead.

*SAM LOWE~The friend who shot the pet snake.

*E.S. JORDAN~Man who bought Nick's first farm.

LENA PERKINS~Midwife who delivered Nick.

JOHN GRINDSTAFF~ A sibling.

MARIE GRINDSTAFF CURD~A sibling

JAKE GRINDSTAFF~A sibling~

DOREEN GRINDSTAFF~ Nick's wife.

NARRATOR~

CORA DUNN~A friend

JANE FARMER~A friend

JUSTICE OF THE PEACE~Marries Nick and Doreen.

MARTHA~ JP'S Wife.

SYNOPSIS~~A true story about Nicholas Grindstaff, who affectionately became know as "Uncle Nick." His first thirty years were somewhat normal even though having lost both parents, by the age of three. He was raised by relatives until he was twenty one. At that time the farm he and his siblings had inherited from his parents, was sold and the money divided. Nick built a house on his fourth and farmed for five years before selling it to E.S. Jordan. He then went West and became a successful sheep herder. Nick was a handsome man, intelligent and hard working. He was an active member in a baptist church, known by all as a good man. In the west, and quite well off financially, Nick found a wife and lived happily until she met a stranger and left. Heartbroken, he again sold the farm and planned to move back East. One night prior, his wife drugged him and robbed him. He moved back East and went to Missouri to a friend for help but was sent back to Tennessee. He returned and acquired a small piece of land and built a hut , living there alone with pets the rest of his life.

# ACT ONE

## Scene one

SETTING: A modest country home with a fireplace, bed, table, chairs and kerosene lamps. Left door and right door. Designated by L and R. Everything dates back to 1851. Beds were often in the living room in poorer families. The midwife, parents and two friends are present on December 26th, 1851. Nicholas Grindstaff has just been born. All attention is on him.

NARRATOR: While whirling snowflakes landed on top of crusted snow on December 26th 1851, Nicholas Grindstaff was making his way into the world. He was the forth child and the third son of Isaac and Mary Grindstaff. He could not know that at the age of three, he would be orphaned by the cruel grasp of death's hand, to find the bitter paths his destiny would lead him on. The first three years of his life were the only ones that afforded him peace and comfort. Afterward, those that followed formed a legend that lives on in Johnson County, Tennessee.

ISAAC: (Walks over to wife's bed, lifts baby.) Welcome to the world , my son.   I hope life's journey is a pleasant one for you. (Sits, holding child. Looks at wife.) Mary get some rest, you've had a hard delivery and you must be weary. Miss Lena and I will take care of this baby.

LENA: (Addresses Mary. Pulls cover up on her.)Oh my yes, Miss Mary, you done wore yo'self out bringing this chile into the world. It was just like he wanted to stay where he was at. (Gives chuckle.) I'll fix some supper for Mr. Grindstaff and the youngin's. (Turns toward door R, looks back.) Ain't got nothin' better to do. (Turns to Isaac.) Gonna fix you and these youngin's some chittlin' bread and beans.

ISAAC: That'll be fine Miss Lena. (Kisses baby.)

CORA: Miss Lena, Can I do something to help? You must be tired too, you've been up since early this morning. I've got potato salad in the spring house, I'll be right back in a minute. (Get's up puts coat on.)

LENA: Oh, Miss Cora, how could I deny this dear family your delicious potato salad?

JANE: (Stands to feet.) I just took a peach cobbler out of the oven right before I left. I'll run right over with it. It was too hot to bring at the time.

ISAAC: (Concerned, Stands holding baby.) Now you dear ladies, I'm much obliged with your kindness but it's so cold outside, I don't want you to get sick, running around in the cold.

JANE: (Waves hand.) Oh, nonsense. Let me hold the baby a minute, and welcome him to the world. (Isaac hands baby to her. She cuddles baby.) You precious little doll, I've got a gift just for you, made it with my own two hands, while we were all waiting for you to get here. Here Cora, I know you can't wait to hold this little bundle. (Hands baby to Cora.) We need to get the food over here. (Turns to Mary who is almost asleep.) Mary get your rest now, we're bringing some more food over and gifts for the baby.

MARY: (Lifts hand weakly.) Thank you my friends so very much. I'm much obliged to all of you. Thank Liza for me, for keeping the children.

JANE: That's what we mountain folk do around here.

CORA: (Cuddles baby.) Oh, you precious little bundle, you are perfect. (Tickles baby's chin.)You're the first baby born in these parts in quite a while. But we really must go now and get the vittles over here, those children will want to come and see their little handsome brother. (Hands baby to Isaac.)

ISAAC: Tell Liza we appreciate her for keeping the youngin's for us.

CORA: (Puts scarf on head.) I will.

JANE: (Slides into coat and covers head with scarf.) I reckon we'd best be going. We'll be back in a little while. We'll bring the children back as we come with the food.

ISAAC: (Lays baby on bed with Mary.) I hope we can repay you ladies in some kind way someday.

CORA: Oh no, you don't owe us a thing. We'll be right back. (Cora and Jane leaves. L )

LENA: (Winds howl outside. Lena Enters, wiping hands on apron. R) You hear that wind a howlin'? Its gonna be a cold one tonight. They callin' fo' snow. I hope it's not a blizzard like last year. The chitlin' bread is just about done Mr. Grindstaff  and the beans are all heated.

ISAAC: (Adds wood to the fireplace.) You're right Miss Lena, they said that down at the store yesterday. Six to twelve inches, maybe more. When I sell some timber next week, I'm going to buy us a radio. (Looks at Mary, takes her hand.) Wouldn't that be nice Honey? We could listen to the news right here at home and some of those shows they talk about down at the store. The kids could learn things about the outside world.

MARY: (Smiles weakly.) I think so. It would be nice.

ISAAC: (Rubs hands excitedly.) And when the President speaks we would listen to him. Yes, we're sure gonna have us a radio. Sure hope the snow don't get so deep I can't do some loggin'. (Turns to Lena.) Miss Lena, I sure would like for you to stay on two or three days and help my wife with the baby and the kids so I can do some loggin'. I will give you one of my smoked hams I've got out there in the smoke house. (Sits in chair. Leans back, crosses legs.

LENA: Why Mr. Grindstaff, you don't have to do that. You know I'd be glad to help out, just like the others are.

ISAAC: Call me Issac, Miss Lena. We've been friends for a long time. I know things have been tough for you since you lost your husband and Mary and me will be there for you. You can always count on us. You've always been a help to us in time of need.

LENA: I know that Mr. Isaac. You mountain folks sure made me glad I moved up here from Georgia.Ain't nobody like you folks here. Don't know what I wouldda done when my Charlie died, if it hadn't been for you all helping with the funeral and the buryin'. Oh, rest in peace, dear Charlie. (Wipes eyes with apron.) Ain't many people helpin' black folk.

ISAAC: We've gotta code here in the mountains, we love people the way we're supposed to.

LENA: I better check on that bread. Cora and Jane and those youngins' gonna come bustin' through that door any minute now. (Leaves room.R)


CURTAIN

# ACT TWO

## Scene One

Setting: December, twenty-one years later in Marie's living room. Tables and chairs are spread throughout the small room. Kerosene lamps, fireplace, pictures and calender on walls. A decorated Christmas tree, occupying space in corner. Outside, falling snow is seen through a small window. An outside door is on the left and an inside door is on the right. Marie, Nick and Jake sit around table drinking coffee and eating cake. More coffee is perking on the iron stand on the fireplace. The faces are sad because it is a time of separation from their childhood days that were so carefree and joyful, until the passing of both parents. Occasional banging outside, as tree limbs warping the house, give a reminder that the wind is blowing fiercely.

NARRATOR: Twenty-one years later in the snow draped mountains of East Tennessee, the siblings have gathered to take care of family business. Seventeen years earlier, the parents passed away, leaving the children orphaned, to be raised by relatives. Nick, the youngest, has grown into a handsome, intelligent young man. He and the siblings have decided to sell the several acres of land they inherited from their parents. They are awaiting the arrival of the oldest brother John who has gone into Carter County to cash the check for the purchase of their land. The money will be divided into fourths to give each an equal share. For the most part, it is a sad day as it seems to sever them from the attachment of their childhood days where they romped and played in fields of clover and sledded down the snow laden hills.

MARIE: (Gets up, pours coffee for all.) I sure wish John would get here, the roads are so bad we should have picked another day to do this. (Sets coffee pot back on iron stand.)

JAKE: (Looks out window.) We should have but John knows how to handle a horse in the snow. Besides Old Riley knows how to trudge through deep snow. (Looks at Nick.) Little brother, you're awfully quite today. Don't fret, we're all feeling a little sad about giving the place up. You got regrets?

NICK: (Deep study.) No, just thinking.

JAKE: Wanna share?

NICK: I wish I remembered something about Ma and Pa. I don't remember one minute I spent with them. I was so young.

MARIE: I guess you're better off that you don't, it just makes this all the more hard to do.

JAKE: (Throws Marie a questioning look.) Marie I thought we all agreed wholeheartedly to do this. You got regrets?

MARIE: (Drops head in hands.) No Jake, it's time to give it up and enjoy a better home or whatever. I just wonder if Ma and Pa would have wanted us to sell it.

JAKE: (Expresses with hands.) If they hadn't they would have surely mentioned it at some point.

MARIE: (Sighs.) I know you're right. I'm being too emotional, us women look at things differently than you men. (Looks at Nick.) What are you going to do with your money Little Brother?

NICK: (Sips coffee, leans back in chair.) Oh I don't know exactly. Maybe buy a farm in the flat lands. Marry. Have a family. Who knows?

JAKE: You've got a family. That's what we are.

NICK: I know. I mean the kind you come home to every night. Look at you three. You all have that already and you've got a home life. You see your kids playing around the fireside at night. I've always wanted that.

JAKE: Don't get too carried away with the idea of marriage. Be sure you're marrying the right one. Think it over, don't jump in the fire. I'm thankful everyday for my Emma and my kids. I reckon we all did land the right ones, right Marie?

MARIE: We did, no doubt. Carl was sent to me from Heaven, no doubt and my children.

NICK: Where is Carl and the kids?

MARIE: He took them sleddin' over on Yancy Hill where we used to go. (Shakes head.) I wish John would get here, I'm a little worried about him, out in this weather on such a long trip.

JAKE: That part of Ma still lives on in you, she

always worried if the head count didn't add up. (Looks at Nick.) Now Little Brother, don't you go hog wild and spend your money on women, no matter how pretty they are.  Spend it on something worth while, like a home or some cattle or something. You're young and young people can do some foolish things.

NICK: Lay off Jake, I'm not the prodigal son. I'm thinkin' I just might buy some land in the valley. I don't like plowin' on hills.

JAKE: Good thinkin' Little Brother. (Slaps Nick on the shoulder.

MARIE: (Knock at door. Rushes to answer.) I sure hope that's John. (Opens door to see John covered in snow.) Mercy sakes, get in here by the fire. Don't mind the snow, get over there by the fire and take that coat off. Are you alright? I've been worried sick about you ever since you left.

JOHN: I'm alright, just freezing. (Takes envelopes out of coat and lays them on the table. Hangs coat and toboggan on rack. Lays gloves by fire.) I had the teller to put it in four envelopes. Count it anyway.

MARIE: (Pours coffee.) Here, get something warm in you. I've got soup if you'll eat some.

JOHN: No coffee's fine. Janice will have supper ready by the time I get home. (Sits at table, sips coffee.) Pass the envelopes out Nick.

NICK: I hope you didn't charge delivery fee.

JOHN: (Grins.)No but I should have in this weather.

MARIE: (Emphatically.) I hope we don't separate from each other now that we've settled things. Remember we are still family.

JAKE: Don't worry 'bout that Sis. We've been through too much together, to forget each other.

MARIE: I know, you know maybe we all ought to pitch in and give the Harrison's some of this money. They were awfully good to take us in and raise us, as their very own.

JOHN: Very well said. (Gets up.) Well I'd best be moseyin' on home. Supper should be about ready. (Addresses Marie.) Tell Carl I'll be by tomorrow to do some trading.

MARIE: I'll tell him. Thanks for going out in this weather to get the check cashed.

JAKE: (Calls across the room.) Yeah, thanks Brother.

NICK: Yeah, me too.

JOHN: Sure thing. (Leaves. L)

MARIE: (Nervously.) I wish Carl would come home and bring those kids in, out of the cold. I'm getting' worried about them now.

JAKE: Sis, you worry too much.

MARIE: There's so many bad things that can

happen. You never know what's going to happen next.

JAKE: (With emphasis.)They can but that doesn't mean they will.

NICK: (Gets up.) I'm going on home, the snow's getting deep out there. (Puts coat and toboggan on and pulls gloves out of pocket.) See you guys tomorrow. Leaves. L)

JAKE: Okay Son. (Reaches for coat and gets up.) Yeah, I'd best be getting on home too. (Looks at Marie.) I'd love to stay and have some of that soup. Sure smells good.

MARIE: Your welcome to stay and eat.

JAKE: I know, thanks anyway. I'll see you tomorrow, I just might do a little tradin' with Carl and John. (Smiling.) Hope you got some of that soup left. Leaves.L)

## CURTAIN

# ACT THREE

## Scene One

Setting: Five years later in Marie's living room. Everything is still the same. Nick and his two brother's are there. The two brothers are playing checkers at a table. Nick impatiently, looks out the window often, pacing the floor. Marie stirs pot on fireplace.

NARRATOR: Five years have passed and Nick has spent it farming on the land he bought. His adventurous soul has led him to sell the farm to E.S. Jordan and move on to a different life. He determines to go west and find an entirely different life. He impatiently waits for Mr. Jordan to come to Marie's house to bring the money, so he can bid his family goodbye and start out on his trek. This seemingly, proves to be, the last time he and his siblings are close.

NICK: (Looking out window. Impatient voice.) I wish Mr. Jordan would hurry up and get here. I aim to be headin' out today. I want to make it past Johnson City before sundown

JAKE: (Looks up from game.) Don't ride that horse too hard, Little Brother, you've got him loaded down. I don't know why you're doing such a foolish thing as this anyway.

NICK: (In disgust.) I don't want to sit here on this mountain and die. What's wrong with wanting to travel on and see some other territory?

MARIE: (Walks over to Nick very concerned.) Honey, you're our baby brother and we care about you. How are we going to know if you're safe out there alone? You've never been away from these hills before. The world out there is a different place than this.

NICK: (Puts arms around Marie.) Don't worry

Sis, I'm going to be okay.

MARIE: (Worried expression.)What if you get robbed? You're carrying a lot of money.

NICK: (Emphatically.) I'm going to be okay. Please don't worry Sis. (Releases hug, steps back.) Sure, I'm still your little brother but I'm a grown man. I need to make my own decisions.

JOHN: (Turns around in chair, left hand on left knee, right arm resting on table. Sincere.) Nick, I don't like this idea either but if you feel you must go, you're twenty one years old and that is considered to be a man. Just please be careful and don't trust just anybody. That's a different world out there. You're not dealing with friends and family.

NICK: (Humbly.) I know John, I promise I'll be careful. (Looks out window again then sits at table.)

MARIE: (Stirring pot.) Nick at least eat some vittles before you go.

NICK: No thanks Sis, I ate a big breakfast. (Knock at door. Nick rushes to answer to see Mr. Jordan.) Come in Mr. Jordan.

E.S. JORDAN: (Steps inside, closes door.)Well son, I've come to settle the deal. (Hands envelope to Nick.) It's all there, count it anyway. (Slaps Nick on shoulder.) Hate to see you leaving these parts. You're a mighty fine young man. We're goin' to miss you at the church. You've been a big help there, even helping to build it and all. Yessir, we hate to see you leave. The Missus sends her love, couldn't hardly say it for cryin'.

MARIE: Won't you have a seat, Mr. Jordan?

E.S. JORDAN: Much obliged Marie, but I've got to be going. Got to run to the store for the Missus. She's doin' some cannin'.

NICK:Thanks,Mr. Jordan.(They shake hands.) Jordan waves slight goodbye. Nick puts money in shirt pocket.)

JAKE: Won't you set a spell E.S.?

JOHN:Yeah, I'll beat you at a game of checkers right quick.

E.S.JORDAN: Sure would like to but the Missus needs some storin' done, I'd better be on my way.(Turns to Nick.) Don't forget us boy, our prayers will be with you. (Nick lifts a hand of farewell. (E.S. Jordan Leaves. L)

NICK: Well if I'm going to make time, I'd best be going. I want to get some road behind me before dark. (Marie is sitting at table, head lowered into hands. Nick goes to her, kisses top of her head.) Bye Bye, Sis. Don't forget, I'll always love you. (Marie nods head, without looking up.)

JAKE: (Gets up. Hugs Nick.) Little Brother,

you look up at the stars every night and you know that's our love shining down on you.

NICK: (Nods. Choked up.)

JOHN: (Gets up, grabs Nick in a bear hug.) Chokes up, says nothing, sits back down. Nick slips out door.)

JAKE: (Looks at Marie who is sobbing aloud. Starts toward her, but sits down hopelessly.)

JOHN: (Sits down at table, looks at Jake with chin resting on hands.)

MARIE: (Voice trembling.) What if we never see him again? This could have been a final goodbye today and it might be. (Wipes eyes with handkerchief.)

JAKE: Now Sis, you've got to quit thinking that way.

MARIE: (Very stern.) Why don't you get real? You hear of things happening everyday and you two act like you're shielded in metal and it can't happen to us.

JAKE:Hey,we don't need to get hasty. We need to stick closer, now that there's fewer of us.

MARIE: I'm sorry. (Crying.) My heart is breaking. We raised him, he's like our own child.

JOHN: Oh, he'll probably be back before he gets out of Tennessee. He's never been away from home before and he ain't gonna like it out there in the big world.

MARIE: It'll just break my heart if he's not here for Christmas.

JAKE: It's like John said, he'll be back before long when he gets a taste of the outside world.


## CURTAIN

# ACT FOUR

## Scene One

Setting: The bedroom of the Justice of the Peace as in the 1850's. The Justice of the Peace is snug in bed with stripped night cap and long gown on. The room holds small night table, desk, lamp, chair, and dresser. The only sound being the rhythm of the JP's snoring.

NARRATOR: Nick Grindstaff is now a young man of thirty five years, a successful sheep herder, who has acquired much, since his move to the West. His good looks, wisdom and success has allowed him to have his pick of the beauty queens who have tried to win his love. He has chosen his lovely Doreen to be his one and only love. It is near midnight on February 14th 1886 and Nick's heart has been struck by cupid's arrow and he is determined to marry.

J.P.:(Lies in a deep sleep, snoring loudly. Knock at door. L Jumps comically with each knock but tries to ignore them. Finally gets up, trudges to door to greet Nick and Doreen.) What can I help you with at this hour of the night?

NICK: (Nervously.) Well Sir, we want to get married.

J.P.: (Looks Doreen over approvingly.) Can't say that I blame you for that.

NICK: Sorry to disturb you but it's important that we get married on Valentine's Day.

J.P. (Yells loudly.) Martha! Come here honey, a couple of lovers are wantin' to get married.

MARTHA: (From back bedroom.)What?

J.P.: Come and be a witness for this marriage!

MARTHA: (Martha appears in gown, curlers in hair. Hugs Doreen.) How sweet, getting married on Valentine's day.

J.P.: Let's get on with this. (Motion to couple.) Stand over here. (Points to Martha.) Right here Martha.

J.P.: What's your names?

NICK: Nick and Doreen.

J.P.: Doreen, now that name's as pretty as you. Nick, do you take this woman to be your lawful wedded wife, to love honor and care for her in sickness and in health, as long as you both shall live?

NICK: (Nervously.) I-I Do.

J.P.:Doreen, do you take this man to be your lawful wedded husband,to love honor and care for him in sickness and health as long as you both shall live?

DOREEN: I do.

J.P. You got a ring?

NICK: No Sir, we just decided a few minutes ago to get married.

J.P. I now pronounce you man and wife. Kiss the Bride. (Nick kisses her.)

NICK: (Takes sizable bill out of his wallet, hands it to the J.P.) Is this alright?

J.P. That's fine. (Turns to Martha.) Write them out a marriage certificate. (Martha sits at desk and writes and hands them the certificate.)

NICK: (Looks adoringly at Doreen.) Much obliged. This has made me a happy man. (Puts arm around her and leads giggling bride to the door. L) Goodbye Sir, Ma'am.

MARTHA: I do hope you have as happy a life, as my man and I have. (Smiles at J.P.)

J.P.: (Hugs Martha with left arm.)Yessir, been married to my gal thirty three years. When we argue, she lets me have her way, every time. That's what you gotta do Son. Keep the Missus happy, at all cost.

NICK: Thanks, I'll remember to do just that.

DOREEN: (Smiling.) Thanks for giving him that advice.

NICK: Goodbye, thanks again. (He and Doreen leave waving goodbye.)

MARTHA: I do hope they will have a happy life together.

J.P.: Well, some do , some don't.

MARTHA: Well, I'm going to bed. Goodnight. (Leaves. R)

J.P.: Goodnight. (Crawls into bed. Snores as curtain closes.)

CURTAIN

## ACT FIVE

### Scene One

Setting: Five years later in Nick and Doreen's living room. The lavish furnishings show Nick's success as a sheep herder.Radio, Chairs, tables, pictures, desk. Everything implicates good taste. Nick sits alone looking downcast.

NARRATOR: Five years have passed and gone taking with it the marital bliss that Nick and Doreen shared at first. Doreen spends much time away from home, causing concern for Nick. He spends many nights alone, after a hard days work on the ranch. Her interest in him, lies only in the money he keeps in the desk drawer and the expensive attire it affords her. He sits pondering over the past years and wondering how he can restore their marriage.

NICK: (Sits in chair, legs crossed, in deep thought, stroking chin. Doreen enters,L dressed in finery. Nick looks up.) Where have you been? Where do you go every night? You're never home when I get here.

DOREEN: (Sarcastically.) Do I have to give account for everything I do? Do I ask you to tell me everything you  do?

NICK: (Stands to feet.) Doreen you know where I am during the day and I'm here where I belong every night. (Grabs her arm.) Talk to me Doreen. What has happened to us? Why do you not want to be with me when I get home?

DOREEN: (pulls away angrily.) Leave me alone.

NICK: Okay. (Stands with hands in pocket, looking out window, in deep thought. Doreen leaves room. R Nick sits at desk, looking through papers. Calculating monthly figures.)

DOREEN: (Enters few minutes later. R Nick looks up. She speaks firmly.) I want a divorce.

NICK: (Stands concerned.) Doreen can't we work this out? I've given you everything you wanted these past five years. You have no reason to want a divorce. Just give it some more time.

DOREEN: After fives years Nick, I think that's time enough. I'll move out tonight. I'll be back later to get my things.

NICK: Is there someone else Doreen? Can he give you what I've given you?

DOREEN: (Whirls around facing him.)Please Nick let's not bring anything into this except a divorce.

NICK: (Emphatically.)Let's not bring a divorce into it. I love you Doreen, as much or more than the day I married you. Please don't go, I'll do whatever I need to,  just to make you happy.

DOREEN: I just want out Nick. Please don't try to stop me, it won't do any good. Just give me a divorce.

NICK: (Pleadingly.) Why?

DOREEN: I don't love you anymore!

NICK: (Quietly.) I see.

DOREEN: (Leaves room, returns quickly with coat and purse.) I'll be back later to get my things. Truth is Nick, I've met someone else. (Nick stands in silence, hands in pocket, watching as Doreen leaves. L)

## CURTAIN

## ACT FIVE

## Scene Two

Setting: The setting is the same, in the living room, just a few days later. Nick is at the desk, working with some business papers. His countenance is sad.

NARRATOR: Nick is all alone now, burying himself into his farm work during the day and busying himself with paperwork at night. His world spins on the axis of agony since Doreen is no longer there. He has acquired a degree of wealth but that no longer brings any degree of happiness. His lingering hope that Doreen will return, is his only companion. His life is a whirlpool of sleepless nights and restless days as he dreads the cycle of each one. In his gullible state he believes Doreen when she comes back, to talk over a cup of drugged tea.

DOREEN: (Comes bursting through door.) Hello Nick, I've decided you are right. We do really need to talk this thing through. I'll just go fix us a good cup of tea and I'll be right back.(Tickles him under chin flirtingly. Starts toward kitchen to fix drugged tea. R)

NICK: (Looks up smiling.)That's great Doreen. I'll be finished here shortly. (Works at desk until Doreen returns.)

DOREEN: (Comes in carrying two cups of tea. Sits his on desk.) Just the way you like it, lightly brewed and one sugar.  (Slides chair close to desk and sits. Sips tea. Watches Nick take first sip.) So, how have you been?

NICK: Not so good, and you?

DOREEN: I was worried about you, that kinda hit you hard. I guess I was just too hasty about it all.

NICK: It was quite a blow.

DOREEN: First let's just drink our tea and then we'll spend a nice quite evening. Perhaps we could take a moonlit walk. Wouldn't that be nice?

NICK: That would be very nice. I'd like that.

DOREEN: You know what I like about moonlit walks down by the mill? It's the honeysuckle fragrance that blows through the night air in a cool refreshing breeze. I always loved the fragrance of the honeysuckle. (Watches Nick as he becomes groggy, stares at him until he slumps over in chair. Gets up to shake him to see if he's out cold. Hurries to desk drawer and takes bag with all of Nick's savings and flees.)

## CURTAIN

# ACT SIX

## Scene One

Setting: A month later back in Missouri, at the home of Benjamin Wilson, a former friend of Nick's. A typical mountain cabin, inhabited by a bachelor, furnished with only necessities, a table, a couple chairs, lamp, animal skins on wall. Benjamin sits, sharpening a knife.

NARRATOR: The worst thing that could have happened to Nick Grindstaff has happened. His wife Doreen has left him, robbing him of his lifetime savings. He sold the ranch for a giveaway price and a horse. Heartbroken, with little money, lonely and depressed, he is ashamed to face his family, after his failure. He goes to a friend in Missouri, Benjamin Wilson, who refuses help and sends him back to Tennessee.

BENJAMIN WILSON: (Sits sharpening knife, singing, 'In the sky, the bright stars glittered, on the bank the pale moon shone. It was from aunt Diana's quilting party, I was seein' Nellie home. I was seein'-----Song interrupted by knock on door. L Answers knock sarcastically) Well if it ain't the wanderer. What are you doin' in these parts with people that ain't good enough for you?

NICK: (Wearily.)Benjamin please, I've always counted you as a friend. With winter comin' on before long, I need a place to stay till I can build me a cabin. I thought maybe you could oblige me for a little while. Believe me, I would have been much better off now, if I'd stayed here but I guess I got the roamin' fever. I always loved everybody here and thought about all of you, wonderin' how everything was going.

BENJAMIN: (Sarcastically.) You get a little money on your hip, selling your Pa's farm and you forsake your family, thinkin' you're too good for us mountain folk and then you come back like a egg suckin dog and expect help from us?

NICK: (Sighs deeply.) Benjamin, it wasn't that way at all. I just wanted to try a different way of life. Didn't you ever wonder what life would be like out there in the world?

BENJAMIN: Us mountain folk tend to our own and we stick with our own. You got above us and went traipsin' off to who knows where, leavin' your family to grieve over you till it finally killed your sister. Never was the same after you left.

NICK: (Wipes brow.) Marie's dead?

BENJAMIN: Yep, buried her two years after you left.

NICK: (Bows head fights back tears.) How about Jake and John and their families?

BENJAMIN: They're all still livin'. Men takes things better than women. Marie was a person that worried a lot.

NICK: (Head bowed.) I'm sorry you feel this way Benjamin. I guess I'd best be movin' on to Tennessee. ( Benjamin gives no response. Goes back to sharpening knife. Nick leaves. L)

CURTAIN

# ACT SEVEN

## Scene One

Setting: Twenty years later in Nick's small cabin. It is sparsely furnished with a table, two chairs, a split log he sleeps on, a stove, a lamp and coffeepot. His pet snake (Rubber.) hangs from rafter. Nick sits drinking coffee.

NARRATOR: Twenty more years have passed since Nick's return to Tennessee. He lived with E.S. Jordan for a while, then decided to build a cabin on Iron Mountain in East Tennessee. He has been a recluse since moving there. He never contacted his family and became known as "Nick the Hermit." Due to his kind ways, in spite of his "Mountain Man" appearance he was affectionately known as "Uncle Nick". He lived with his dog Panter and a pet rattlesnake. His defense weapons were a barlow knife, an axe and a hickory stick. His time was spent clearing land building fences, raising a garden, and gathering roots and herbs to trade for supplies. Although he isolated himself and looked rugged, in his many layers of old clothes and long hair, no one was afraid of him because of his kindness. He kept much to himself, in his cabin on the highest peak of the mountain, where the Johnson and Carter County dividing lines meet. It could naturally be assumed that many times during summer breezes, or long winter nights, Nick would often wonder where his one time love, Doreen could be. Perhaps, the good memories of her in their first years of marriage were a consolation to him. On the other hand, maybe they were to painful to recollect. Either way, it was something he never mentioned, keeping them hidden in the closets of his mind.

NICK: (A knock sounds. Nick takes another sip of coffee before answering. Opens door.) Well, if it's not ol' Sam. Come in Sam, good to see you. Want some coffee? Have a seat.

SAM: (Sits in opposite chair.) No, much obliged though, had some biscuits and side meat. This morning, made me some side meat gravy. Nothing like good ol' brown side meat gravy.

NICK: That's some good eatin' alright. You got firewood in for the winter? (Sips coffee.)

SAM: (Scoots chair back, crosses legs.) Been working all summer on it. They're sayin' this winter's goin' to be a rough one. Wooly worms got wide black bands and onion skins are thicker than usual. Two sure signs.

NICK: Me too. These October mornin's already getting' a bit chilly, if you ask me. I built a fire one mornin' already.

SAM: Yeah, won't be surprised if there's a frost on the ground one of these mornin's real soon. They said down at the store some place in the West already was getting snow.

NICK: (Looks down saddened at the mention of the west. Sips coffee, holds cup in both hands.) You goin' to plant tobacco next spring?

SAM: Just a few stalks just for my on chewin'. Want me to plant a few extra for you ?

NICK: That would be might neighborly of you, if you would.

SAM: (Looks up gasps in fear, aims pistol.) Nick! there's a blasted rattlesnake on that rafter!

NICK: (Lowers Sam's arm.) Don't shoot, that's my pet, he does no harm. I've kept Panter from killing him lots of times. He's been here almost as long as I have. Found him in here, when he was just a baby.

SAM: (Looks at Nick astonished.) Nick do you hear yourself? That thing could kill you in your sleep.

NICK: That snake has kept my feet warm many cold nights. (Nick gets up, heads for door.) Better check on Panter, think I heard some coyotes out there last night. (Goes outside. L)

SAM: (Gets up, aims gun at rattler.) You blasted varmit, I'm bringin' you down, right now. (Fires shot, snake falls dead to floor.)

NICK: (Runs in breathless.) What's goin' on here? (Looks at snake.) You shot my snake? I told you that snake was harmless.

SAM: Yep, he is, now. (Puts gun back in holster.)

NICK:(Emphatically.) Sam, that snake's been better to me than a lot of people. Got a better heart in him than some I've seen.

SAM: I couldn't leave here worryin' about that thing killin' you and us findin' you. Don't you feel hard toward me. I meant it for your own good.

NICK: (Expresses with hands.) You just don't understand the nature of the wild, Sam. You don't harm them, they don't harm you.

SAM: (Stern voice.) Lot's of folk here in the mountains are laying in their graves, because of rattlesnake and copperhead bites.

NICK: Well, we've been friends too long to end it over this. Even though I do hate that you did this. (Looks sadly at snake.)

SAM: Well on that note, I'd best be goin'. (Starts toward the door. R)

NICK: (Loudly.)Don't shoot my dog on your way out! (Gives a slight wave with hand.)

SAM: (Makes face at Nick and leaves. L)

CURTAIN

## ACT EIGHT

### Scene One

Setting: Almost a year later, July 25, 1923. Nick is lying on the floor lifeless. There are no signs of struggle. A coffee cup half full, sits on the table. A plate of food, hardly any eaten, sits beside the cup. Loud knocking outside can be heard as Baxter McEwen, a neighbor, pounds consistently on the door.

BAXTER: (Heard from outside.) Nick, come on open up. The old Lady sent you some rolls and stew. She wanted you to eat this while it's hot. If you don't answer, I'm coming in anyway, got to set this stuff somewhere. (Shoves door open. Sees Nick lying on floor.) Jeminy Crickets! Who would have thought this? (Sets food down and kneels beside Nick. Shakes body and rolls his lifeless form over.) I gotta get somebody in here. (Stands up, looks at body. Leaves L)

NARRATOR: And so ends the lonely heartbroken life of Nick Grindstaff, known to all as, "Nick the Hermit." A kind gentleman, who never did harm to anyone but took the cruel brunt of several. It was believed his decomposed body had lain in state for four days, with his faithful dog, Panter guarding his master's body. Panter had to be tied before men could carry Nick's body out for burial. Nick was buried on the mountain peak where he lived the last thirty or forty years of his life. A gravestone was erected so passersby would remember him. Today, the Appalachian Trail passes by the area. The Cherokee National Forrest maintains the monument that marks Nick's burial site. Rest in Peace, good Buddy.